THIS BOOK

Belongs to

_____

_____

"Success is going from failure to failure without losing your enthusiasm."

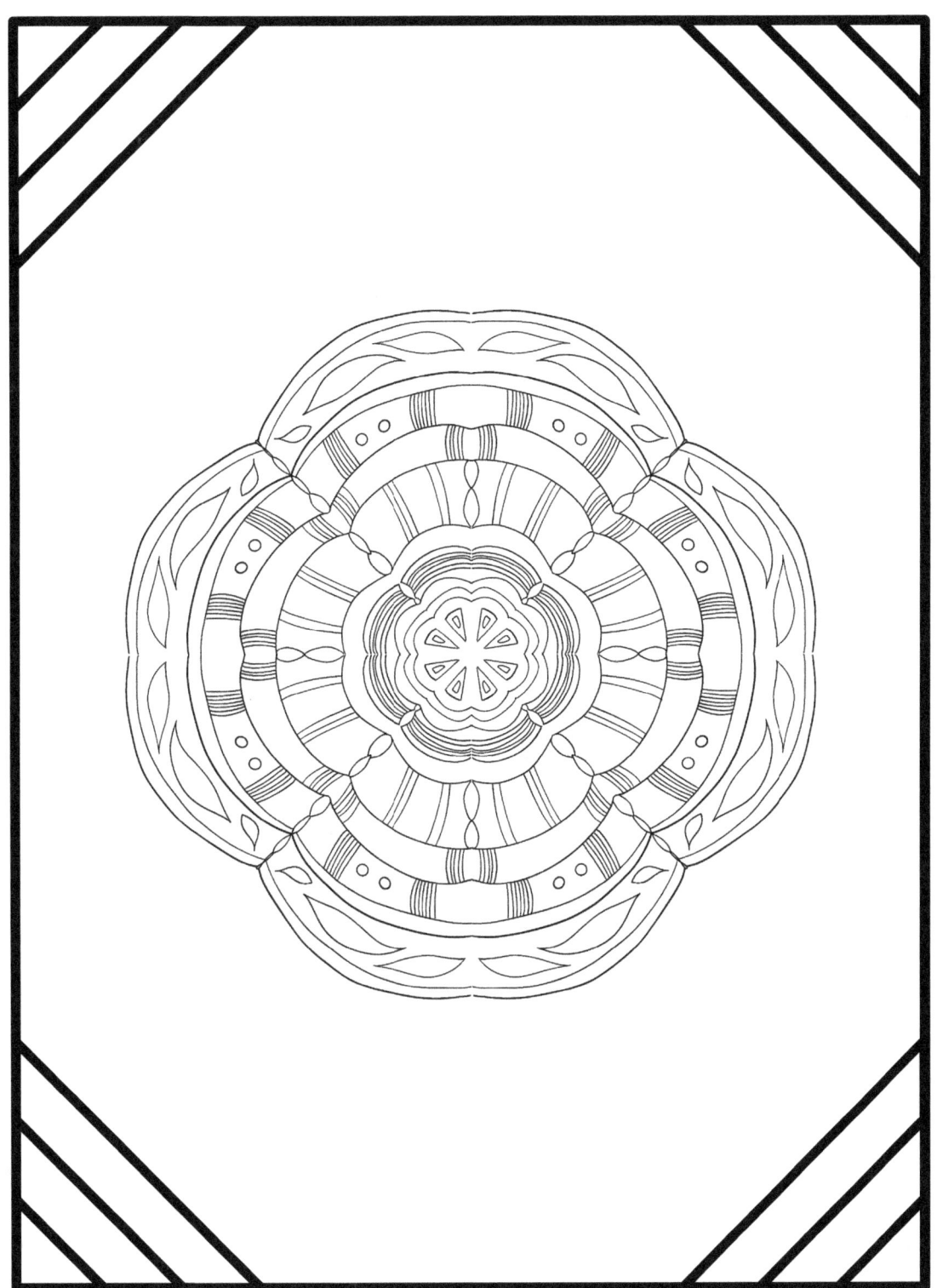

"If you can dream it,
you can achieve it."

"The only way to do great work is to love what you do."

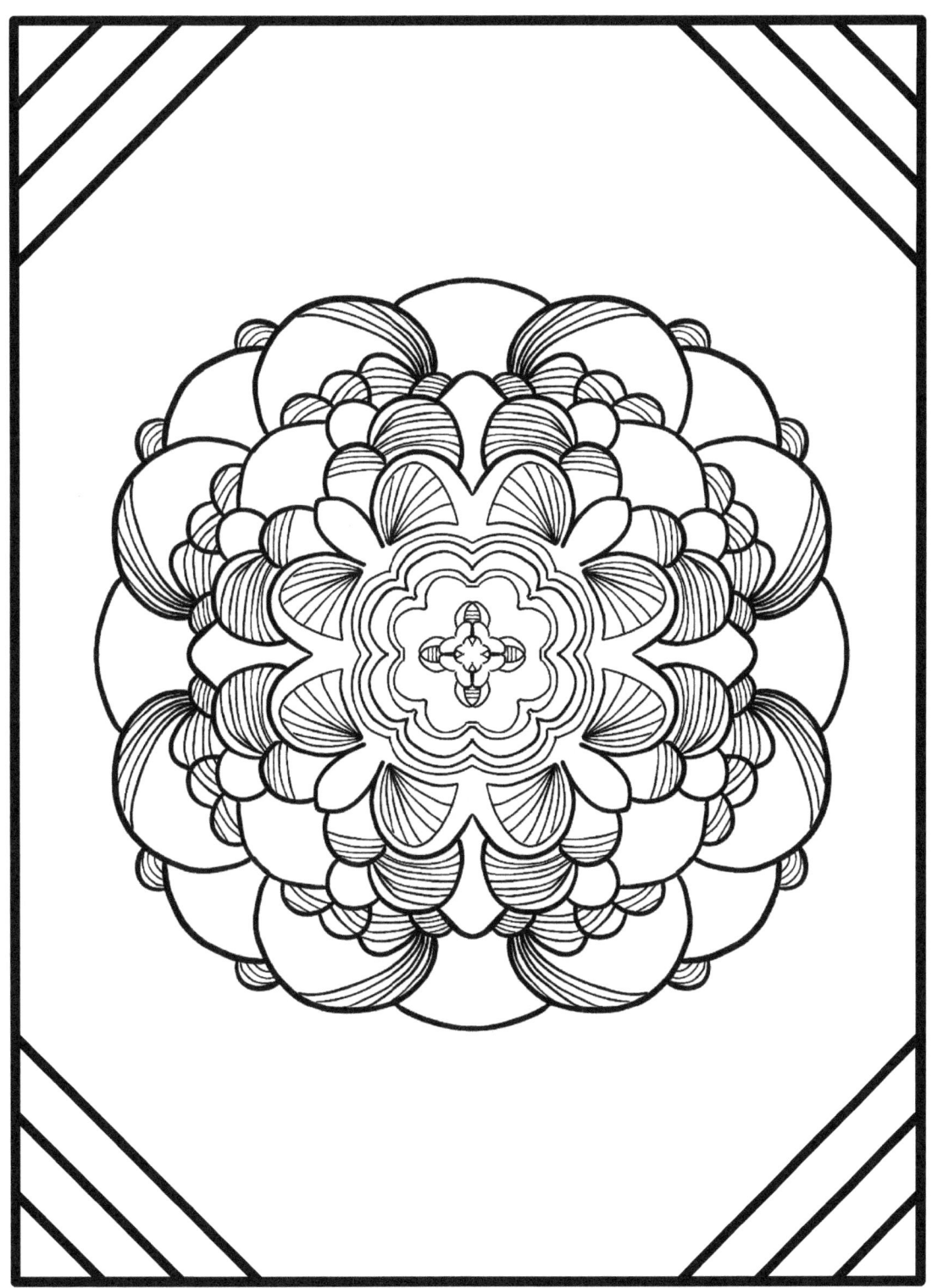

"When everything seems to be going against you, remember that the airplane takes off against the wind, not with it."

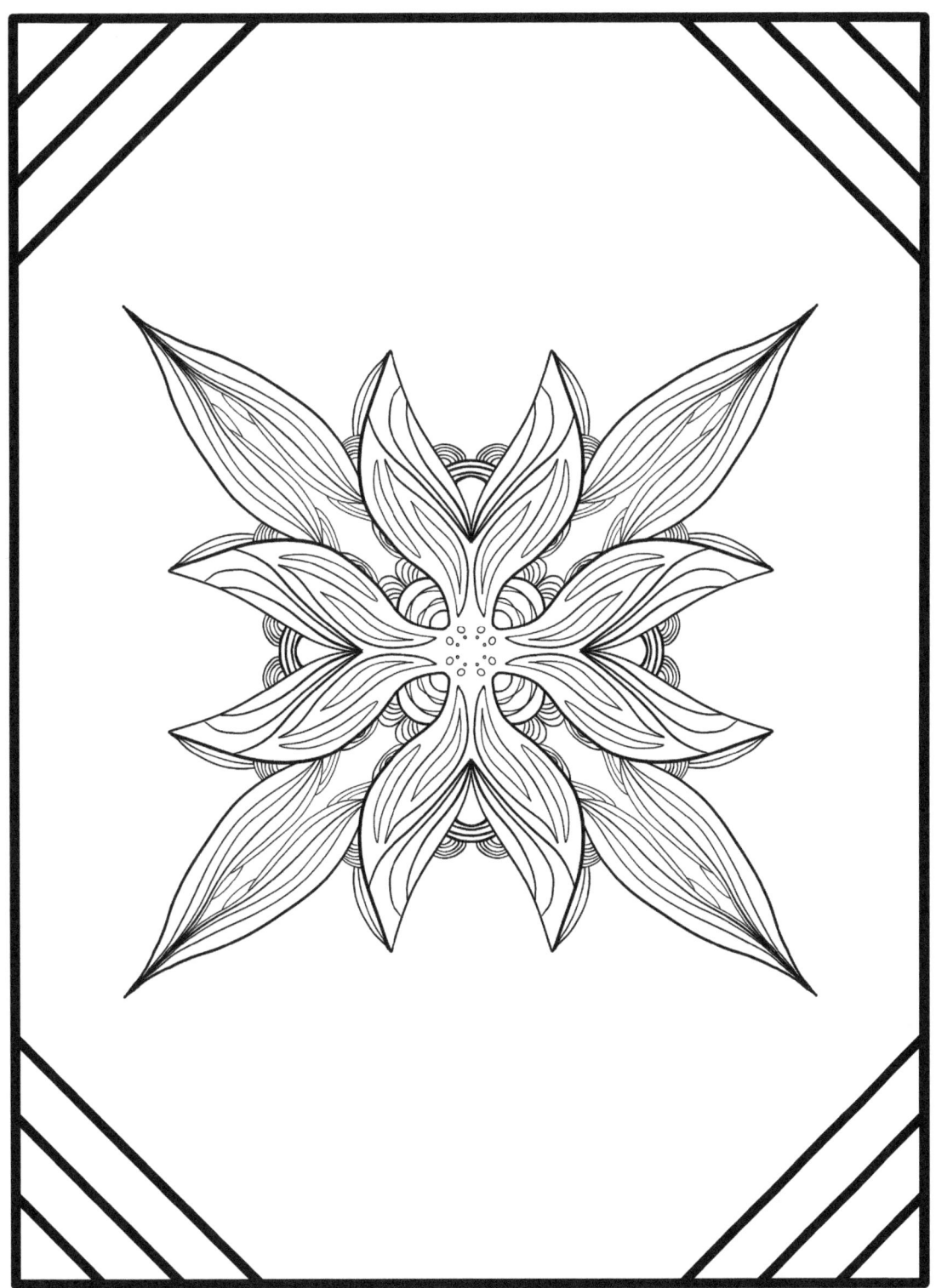

"Life is what we make it, always has been, always will be."

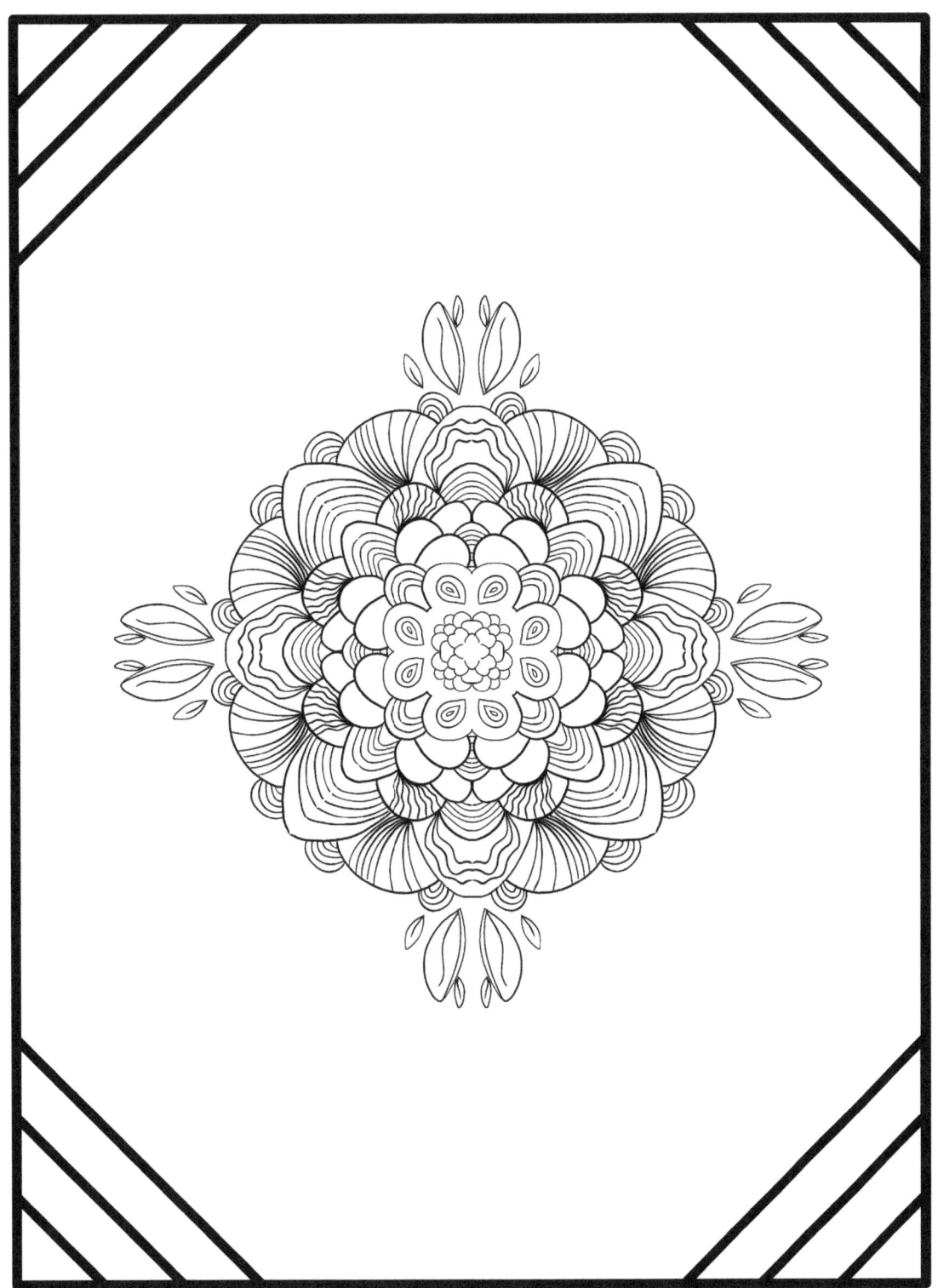

"You may be disappointed if you fail, but you are doomed if you don't try."

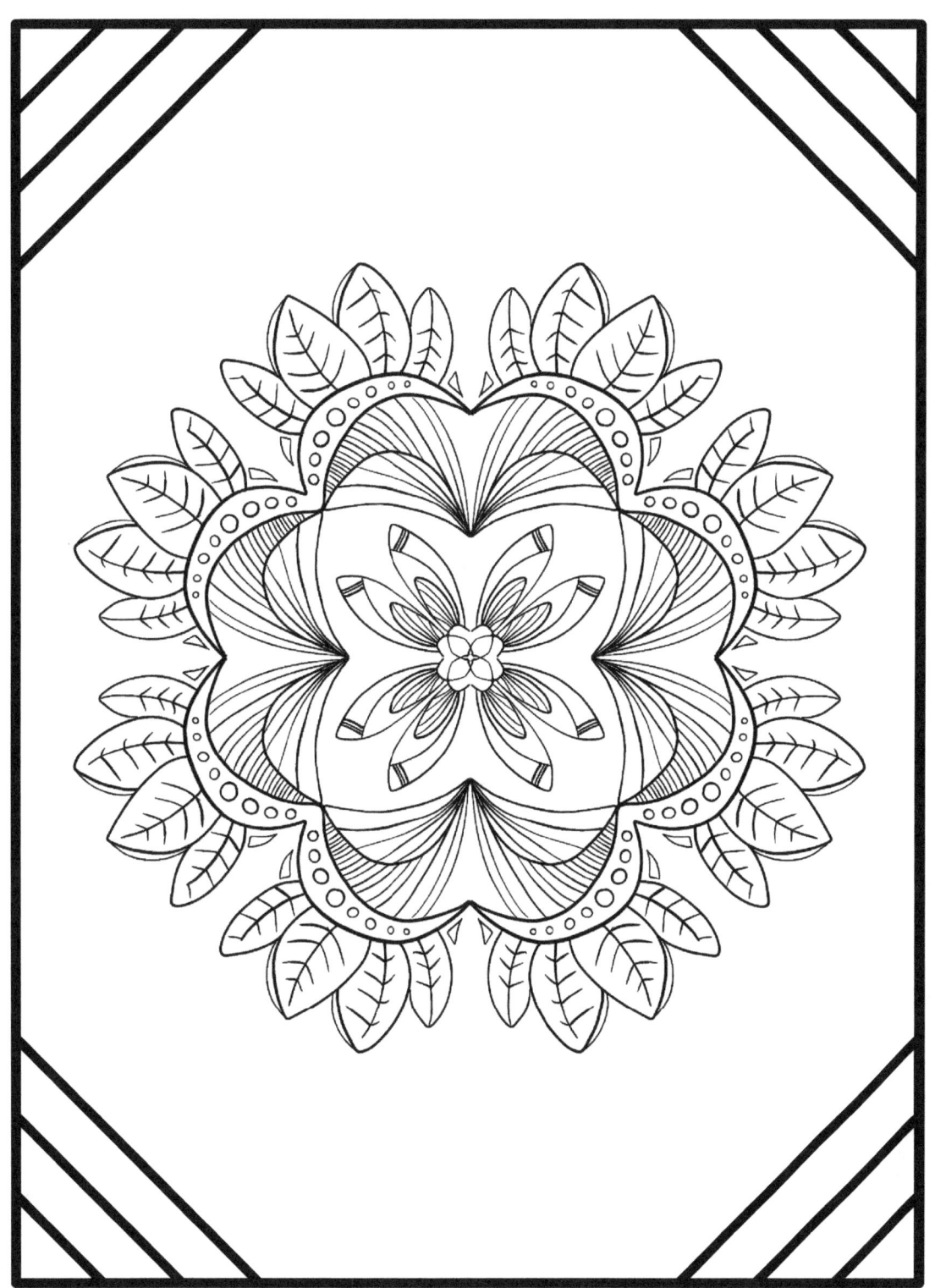

"Dream big and dare to fail."

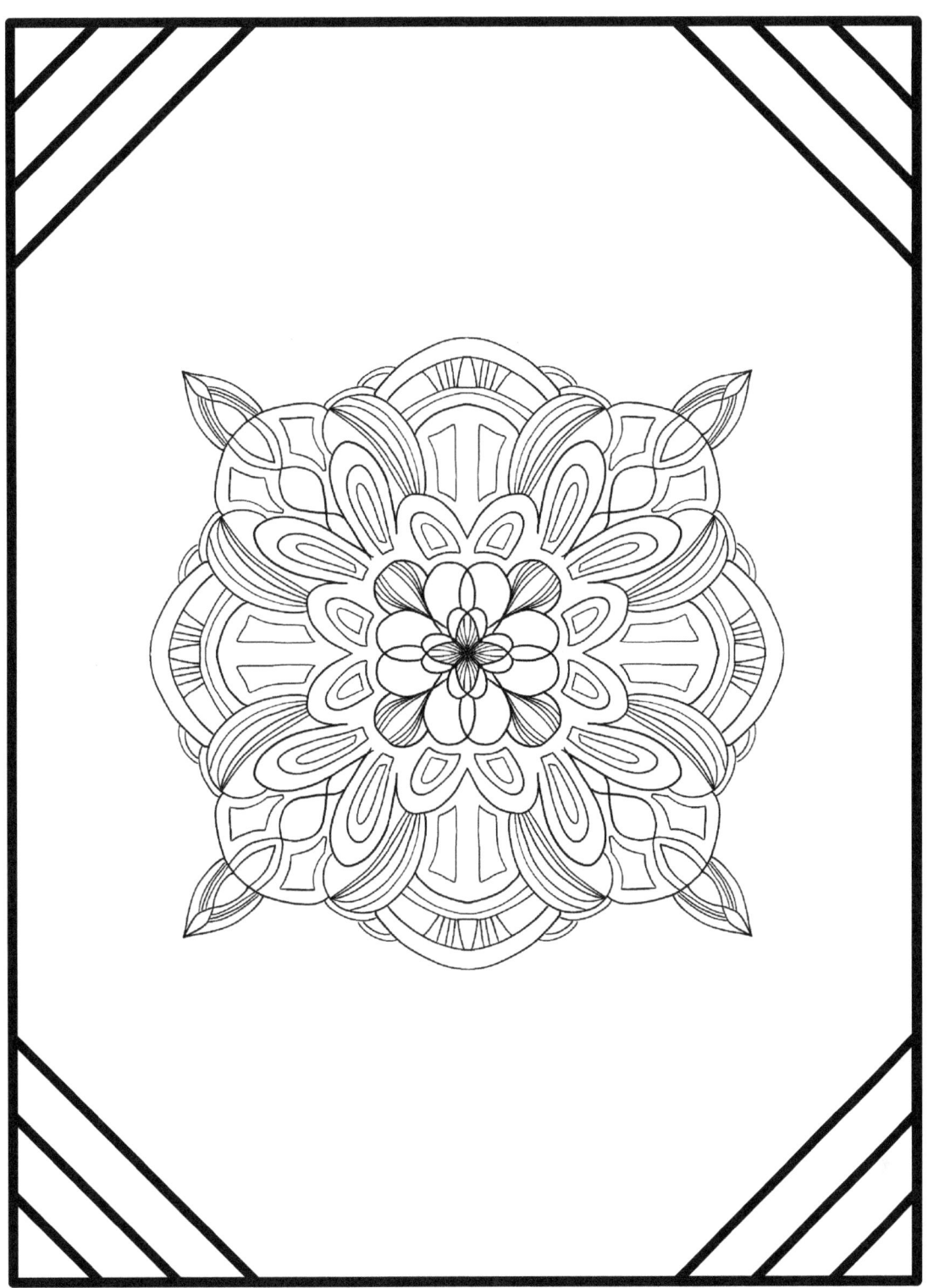

"It does not matter how slowly you go as long as you do not stop."

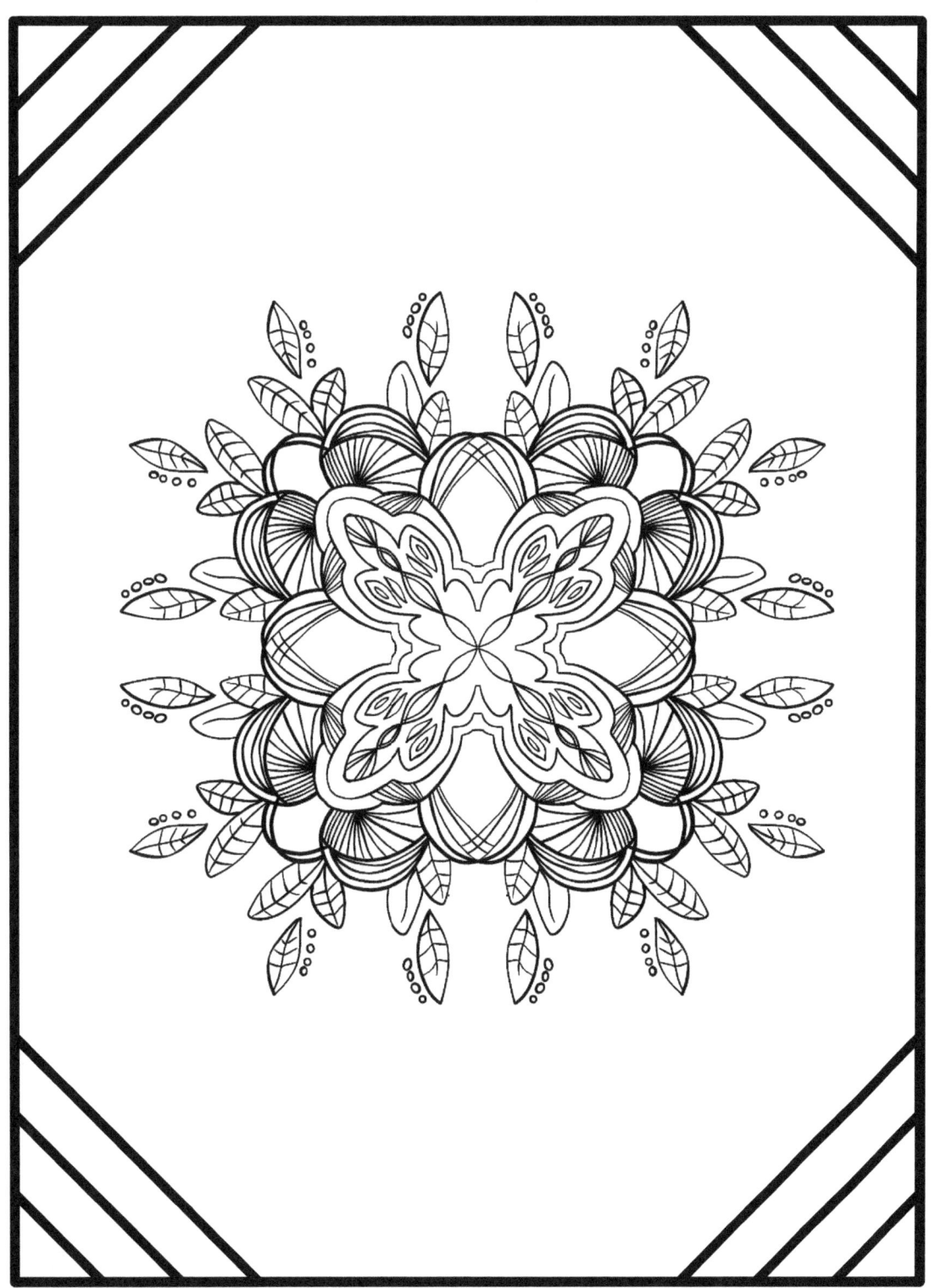

"Build your own dreams, or someone else will hire you to build theirs."

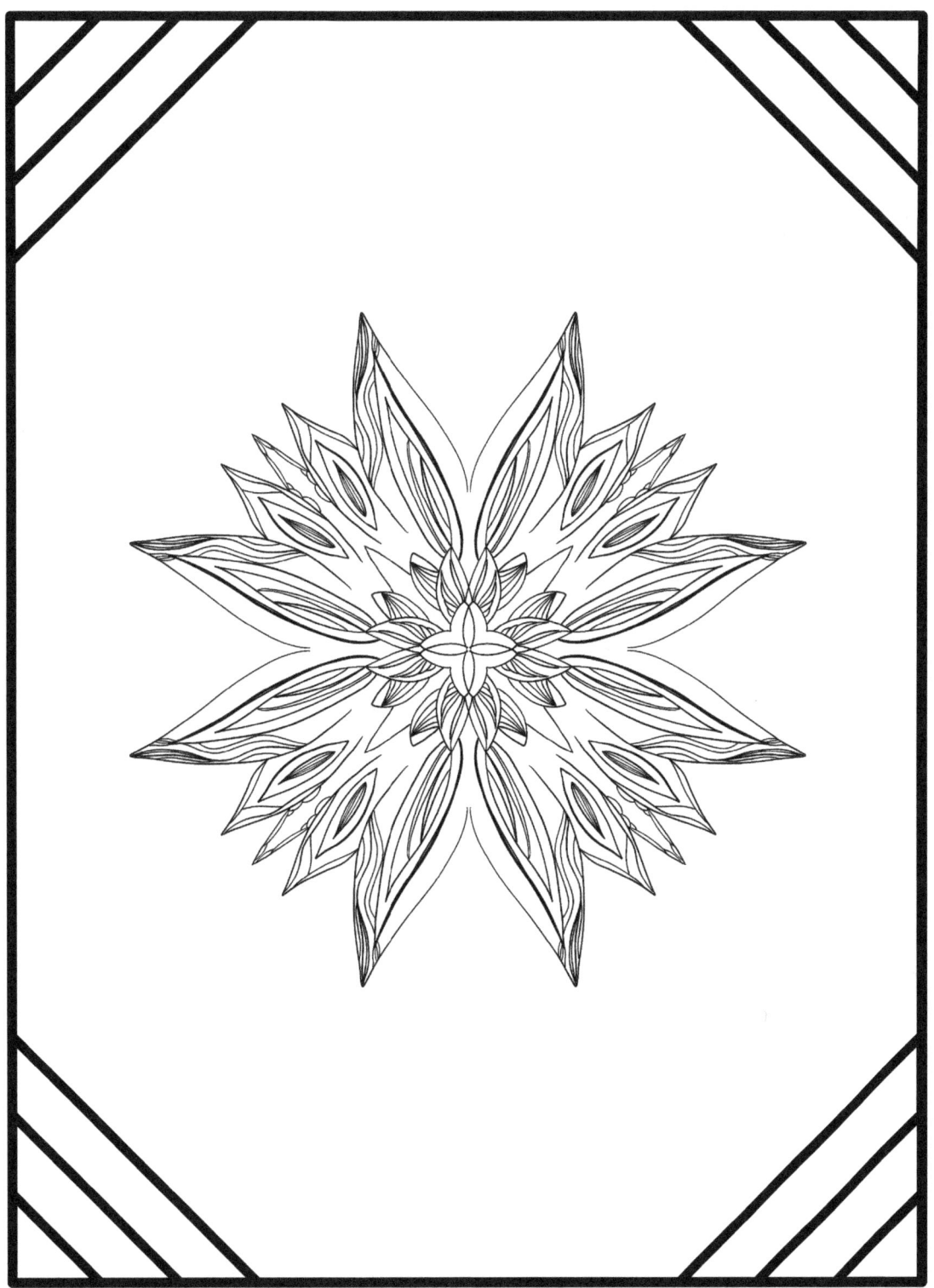

" I would rather die of passion than of boredom."

"I didn't fail the test. I just found 100 ways to do it wrong."

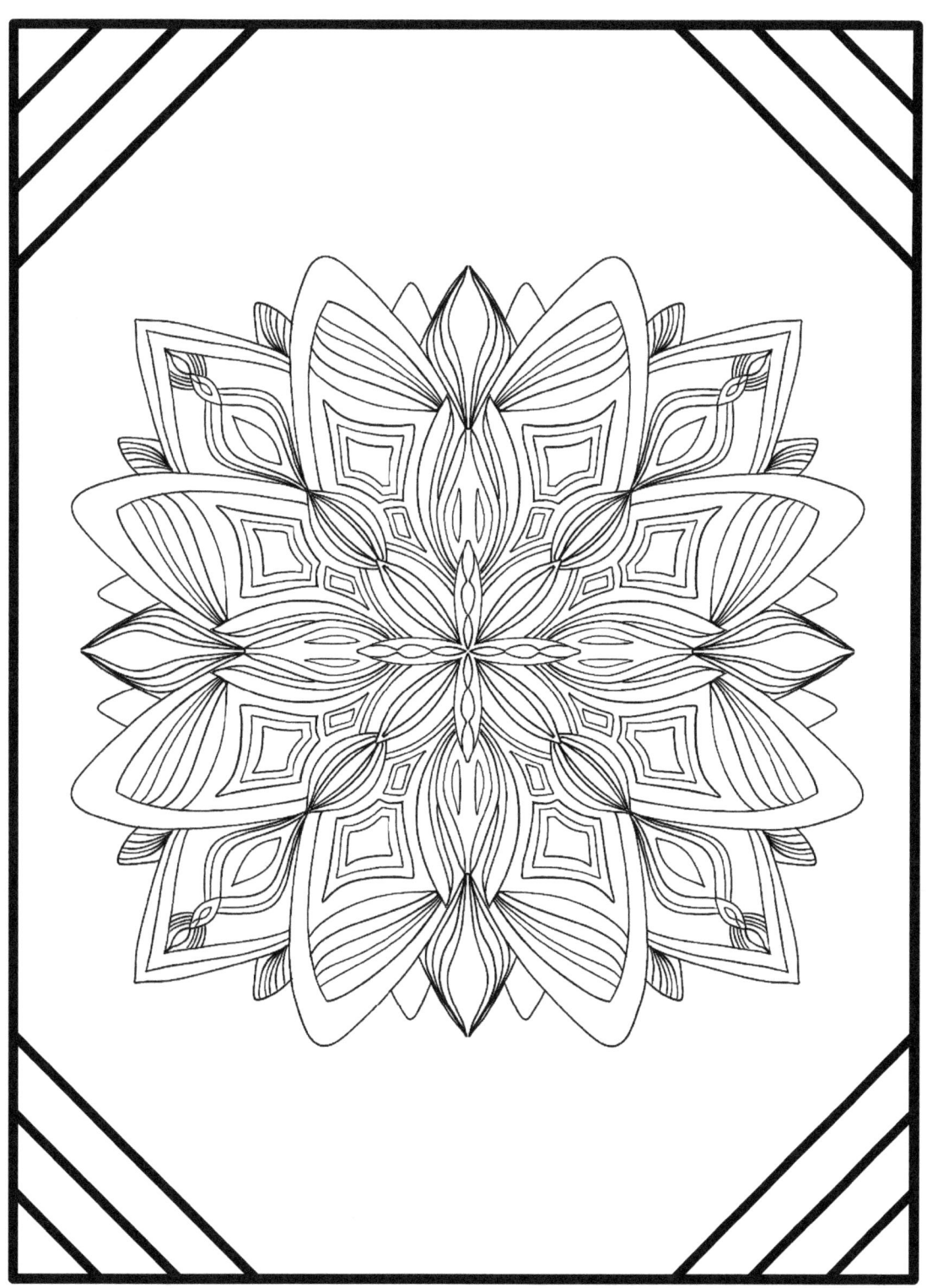

" Limitations live only in our minds. But if we use our imaginations, our possibilities become limitless."

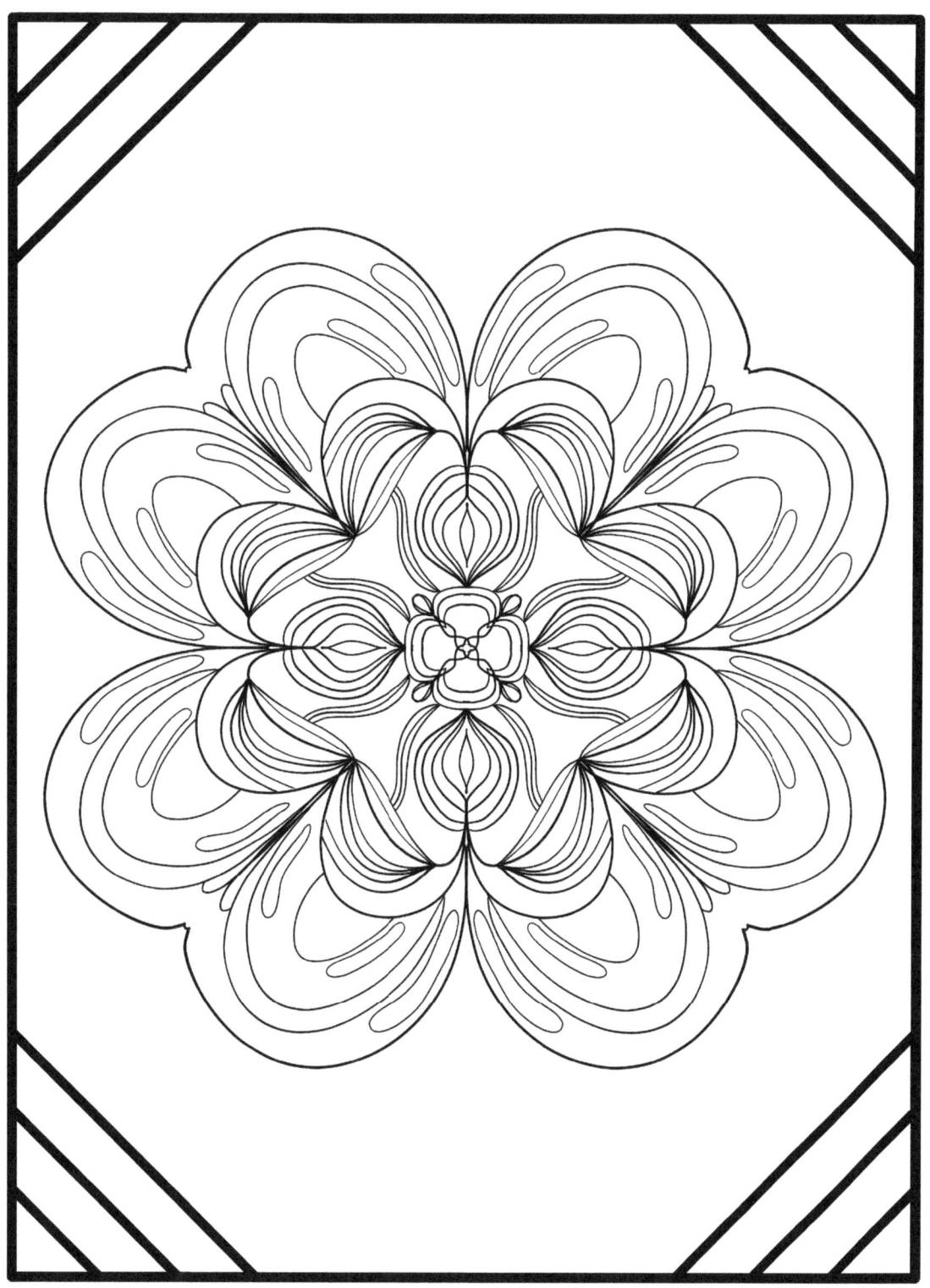

"Challenges are what make life interesting and overcoming them is what makes life meaningful."

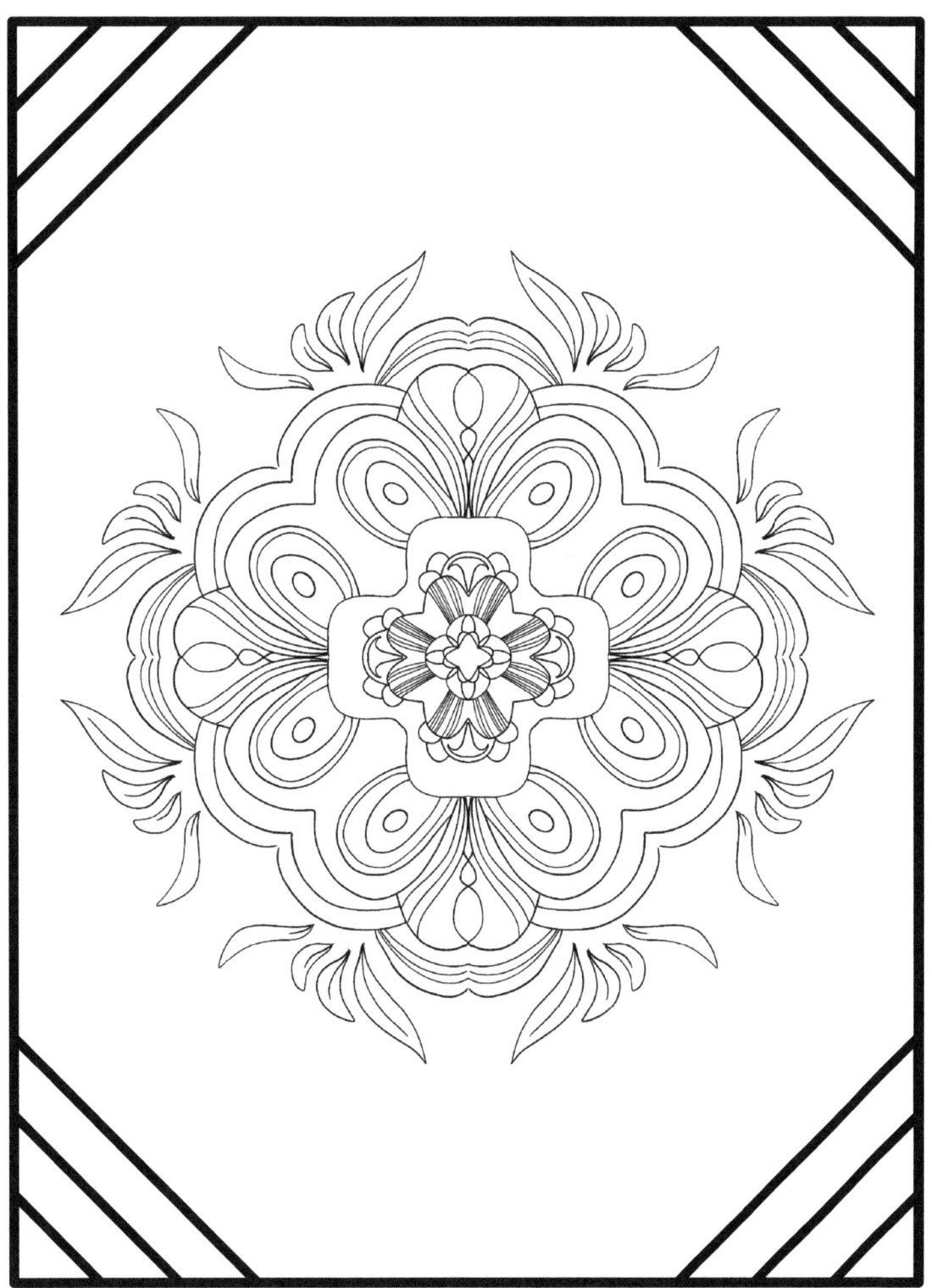

"Too many of us are not living our dreams because we are living our fears."

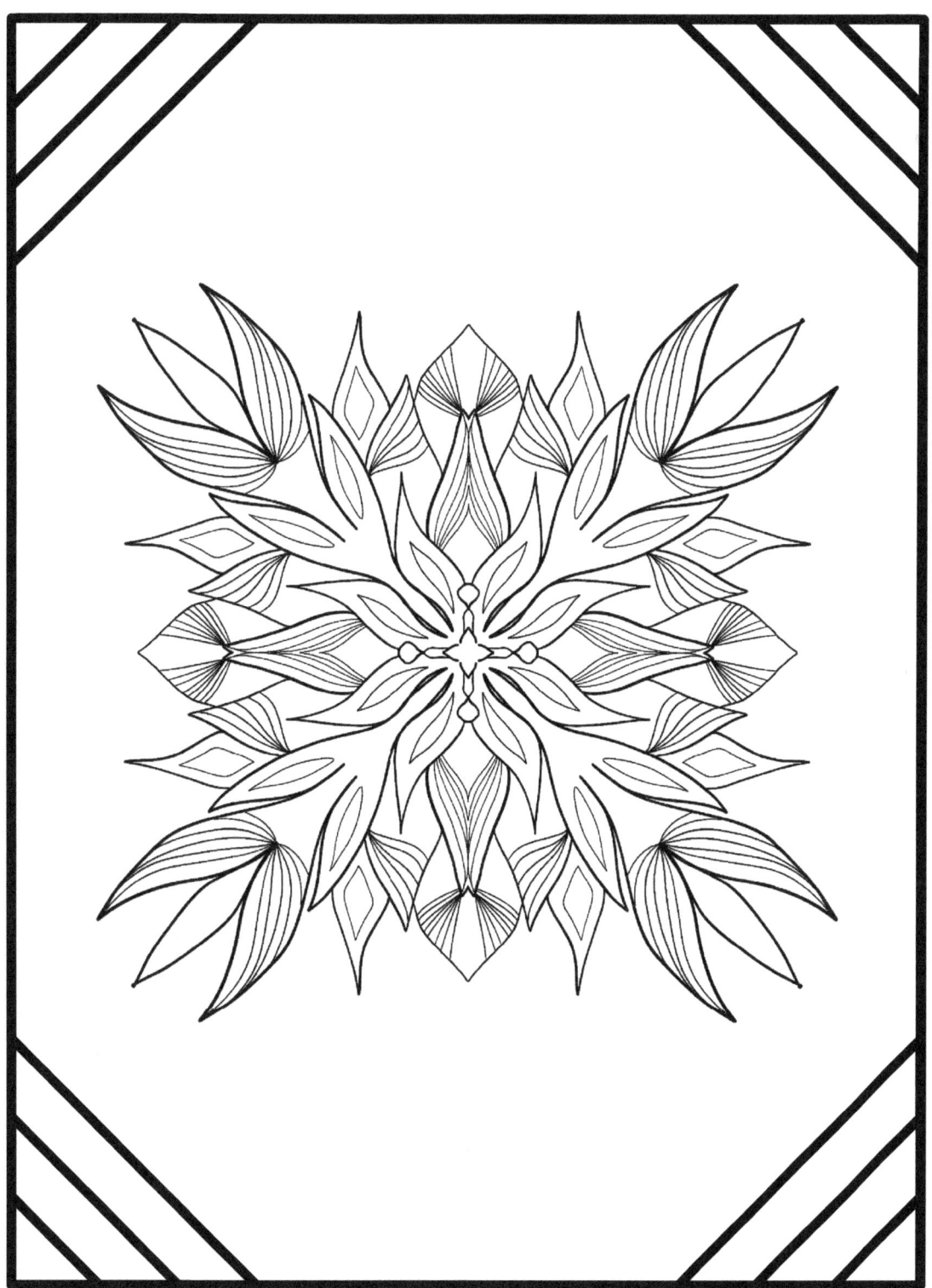

" If you're offered a seat on a rocket ship, don't ask what seat! Just get on."

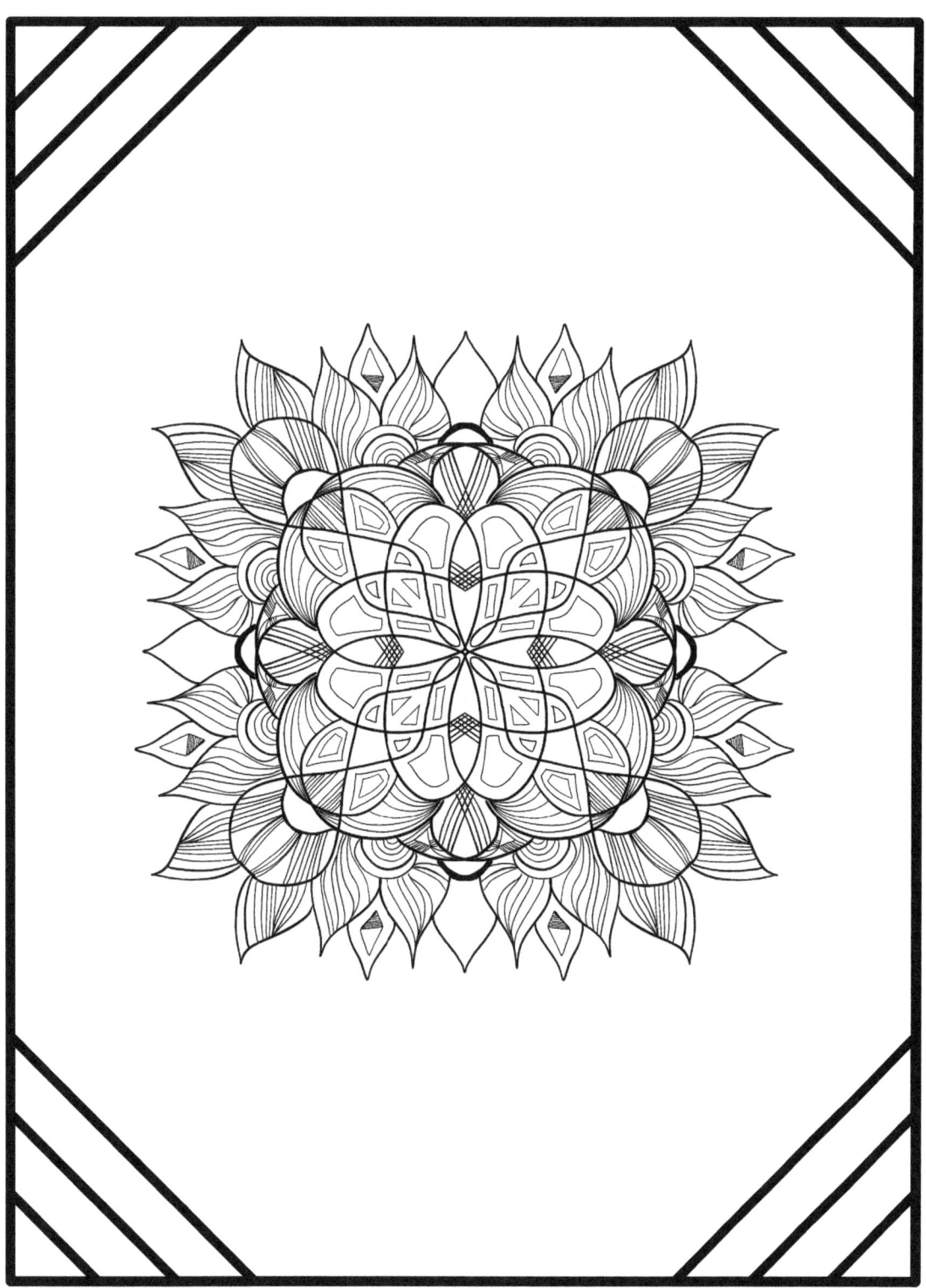

"Happiness is not something readymade. It comes from your own actions."